Tell Me How You Feel

Linda Johns

illustrated by Rosario Valderrama

I feel HAPPY.
I giggle and squeal.

But tell me, tell me, how do **you** feel?

I feel BRAVE.
It's no big deal.

But tell me, tell me,
how do **you** feel?

I feel SCARED.
This feeling is so real.

But tell me, tell me,
how do **you** feel?

I feel PROUD.
I could do a cartwheel.

But tell me, tell me,
how do **you** feel?
Do **you** like this Ferris wheel?